Trombone 1

# CHRISTMAS BRASS QUARTETS

## Two Trumpets in B-flat and Two Trombones

*intermediate level*

CANADIAN BRASS

ISBN 978-1-70517-576-7

EXCLUSIVELY DISTRIBUTED BY

HAL•LEONARD®

www.canadianbrass.com
www.halleonard.com

World headquarters, contact:
**Hal Leonard**
7777 West Bluemound Road
Milwaukee, WI 53213
Email: info@halleonard.com

In Europe, contact:
**Hal Leonard Europe Limited**
1 Red Place
London, W1K 6PL
Email: info@halleonardeurope.com

In Australia, contact:
**Hal Leonard Australia Pty. Ltd.**
4 Lentara Court
Cheltenham, Victoria, 3192 Australia
Email: info@halleonard.com.au

# CONTENTS

# ANGELS WE HAVE HEARD ON HIGH

Traditional French Carol

# DING, DONG! MERRILY ON HIGH

Traditional French Carol

# THE FIRST NOEL

17th Century English Carol
Music from W. Sandys' *Christmas Carols*

# GO, TELL IT ON THE MOUNTAIN

African-American Spiritual

# GOD REST YE MERRY, GENTLEMEN

Traditional English Carol

# HARK! THE HERALD ANGELS SING

Music by Felix Mendelssohn-Bartholdy

# IN DULCI JUBILO

14th Century German Melody

# JOY TO THE WORLD

Music by George Frideric Handel